W9-BAH-102

NEW ENGLAND
PATRIOTS

by Mary Motzko

Published by ABDO Publishing Company, 8000 West 78th Street, Edina, Minnesota 55439. Copyright © 2011 by Abdo Consulting Group, Inc. International copyrights reserved in all countries. No part of this book may be reproduced in any form without written permission from the publisher. SportsZone™ is a trademark and logo of ABDO Publishing Company.

Printed in the United States of America,
North Mankato, Minnesota
062010
092010

 THIS BOOK CONTAINS AT LEAST 10% RECYCLED MATERIALS.

Editor: Matt Tustison
Copy Editor: Nicholas Cafarelli
Interior Design and Production: Kazuko Collins
Cover Design: Christa Schneider

Photo Credits: Robert E. Klein/AP Images, cover; AP Images, title page, 12, 15, 16, 18, 20, 22, 42 (top and middle); Amy Sancetta/AP Images, 4, 34, 43 (middle); Elise Amendola/AP Images, 7; Doug Mills/AP Images, 9, 28; NFL Photos/ AP Images, 11, 24, 44; Ray Stubblebine/AP Images, 27, 42 (bottom); Elaine Thompson/AP Images, 31; Steven Senne/AP Images, 33, 43 (top); Dave Martin/ AP Images, 37; Julie Jacobson/AP Images, 38; Stephan Savoia/AP Images, 41, 43 (bottom); Robert E. Klein/AP Images, 47

Library of Congress Cataloging-in-Publication Data
Motzko, Mary, 1980-
  New England Patriots / Mary Motzko.
      p. cm. — (Inside the NFL)
  ISBN 978-1-61714-019-8
  1. New England Patriots (Football team—History—Juvenile literature. I. Title.
  GV956.N36M68 2010
  796.332'640974461—dc22
                                    2010017020

TABLE OF CONTENTS

CHAPTER 1

CHAMPIONS AT LAST

Before the start of the 2001 season, the New England Patriots were not considered a Super Bowl contender. They were coming off a 5–11 season. They were not among the favorites to win their own division, let alone professional sports' biggest game. But they would make one of the most unlikely playoff runs in National Football League (NFL) history.

Some incredible things happened for the Patriots in that 2001 season. Second-year quarterback Tom Brady was forced into a leadership role after starter Drew Bledsoe was injured in the second game. Bledsoe suffered internal bleeding after he was hit hard by New York Jets linebacker Mo Lewis. Brady stepped in and, after a shaky couple of outings, played better than anyone could have expected. After all, the Patriots had not selected him until the sixth round of the NFL Draft in April 2000. He had attempted just three passes in his rookie NFL season.

LINEBACKER TEDY BRUSCHI KISSES THE TITLE TROPHY AFTER THE PATRIOTS UPSET THE RAMS 20–17 IN FEBRUARY 2002 FOR THEIR FIRST SUPER BOWL WIN.

"TUCK RULE GAME"

The Patriots' 16–13 overtime playoff win over the Oakland Raiders on January 19, 2002, is often referred to as the "tuck rule game." The game-changing play involved a little-known NFL rule introduced in 1999.

On the key play late in the fourth quarter, New England quarterback Tom Brady lost the ball after being hit by Oakland cornerback Charles Woodson. Raiders linebacker Greg Biekert made the recovery.

Officials originally ruled that the ball was Oakland's. But after a video replay, officials said the play was a forward pass attempt by Brady and thus an incompletion. Referee Walt Coleman said the "tuck rule" applied because Brady's arm was moving forward before he decided not to release the ball and Brady had not "tucked" the ball into his body.

Thus, the original call was overturned. The Patriots took advantage of their second opportunity by forcing overtime and then winning.

But Brady took his big opportunity in 2001 and ran with it. He would start the rest of the regular season. At age 24, he played with maturity beyond his years. The Patriots finished 11–5 and tied for the American Football Conference (AFC) East Division title with the Miami Dolphins. Brady threw for 18 touchdowns with just 12 interceptions.

But advancing through the NFL playoffs is almost never easy. Brady and the 2001 New England team found that out.

The first test was a snowy game against the Oakland Raiders at the Patriots' home, Foxboro Stadium in Foxborough, Massachusetts. The Patriots received some major assistance from the officials. A play late in the game that was originally ruled a fumble by Brady was overturned after a

THE PATRIOTS' TOM BRADY LOSES THE BALL AS THE RAIDERS' GREG BIEKERT, *LEFT*, AND CHARLES WOODSON LOOK ON DURING A PLAYOFF GAME IN JANUARY 2002. OAKLAND RECOVERED THE BALL, BUT OFFICIALS OVERTURNED THE CALL ON THE "TUCK RULE PLAY."

video review. The officials determined that it was actually an incomplete pass. Oakland had recovered the ball. If the first ruling had stood, the Raiders could have run out the clock and won.

Instead, the Patriots had a second chance. They made the most of it when Adam Vinatieri, kicking into the wind and snow, made a 45-yard field goal with 27 seconds remaining. This tied the score at 13–13. In overtime, Vinatieri converted a 23-yard kick to give New England a 16–13 victory.

The Patriots visited the Pittsburgh Steelers in the AFC Championship Game. Pittsburgh had gone 13–3 in the regular season. New England's chances of winning seemed to take a terrible blow when Brady went down with a knee injury in the second quarter. No matter. Bledsoe, who had been cleared to play several weeks previously, stepped in for Brady, just as Brady had done for Bledsoe. Bledsoe threw a touchdown pass to help the Patriots win 24–17. Their fairy-tale season would continue.

BRADY AND BLEDSOE

New England selected Drew Bledsoe as the No. 1 overall pick in the 1993 NFL Draft. He excelled for several seasons as the Patriots' starting quarterback but was forced out of the lineup with an injury in Week 2 of the 2001 season. In his absence, backup Tom Brady took over as the starter. Even when Bledsoe was cleared to return later in the season, Brady remained the starter. Bledsoe accepted his role. He also remained ready to jump back into action. This benefited the Patriots in the AFC title game. When Brady suffered a knee injury, Bledsoe led the Patriots past the Steelers. After the season, New England traded Bledsoe to the Buffalo Bills for a first-round draft pick.

The Patriots entered Super Bowl XXXVI on February 3, 2002, at the Superdome in New Orleans, Louisiana, as 14-point underdogs to the St. Louis Rams. St. Louis' high-powered offense was billed as the "Greatest Show on Turf." Quarterback Kurt Warner and running back Marshall Faulk were the leaders. The Rams had finished with an NFL-best 14–2 regular-season record. St. Louis had won a Super Bowl just two years previously with a 23–16 victory over the Tennessee Titans.

But the Patriots came ready to play. New England cornerback Ty Law intercepted a pass from Warner and returned it 47 yards for a touchdown in the second quarter. Brady—back from his injury—then connected with David Patten on an 8-yard touchdown pass. The surprising Patriots led 14–3 at halftime.

NEW ENGLAND'S TOM BRADY PASSES IN SUPER BOWL XXXVI AGAINST ST. LOUIS. THE SECOND-YEAR PLAYER WAS CALM IN THE BIG GAME.

New England continued to lead the game as the third quarter progressed. Otis Smith's interception of a pass by Warner set up a 37-yard field goal by Vinatieri. The Patriots took a 17–3 lead.

But the Rams had an explosive offense and could get back into games quickly. That is exactly what happened. Warner scored on a 2-yard keeper to cut the Rams' deficit to 17–10 with 9:31 remaining in the game.

Then, Warner threw a 26-yard touchdown pass to Ricky Proehl with 1:30 left. The extra point tied the score at 17–17.

It would have been easy for the Patriots to become discouraged. But the team, behind Brady, had been mentally tough all season. Working with no time-outs, Brady completed throws to J. R. Redmond, Troy Brown, and Jermaine Wiggins. The last pass went for 6 yards and put the ball on the Rams' 30-yard line. Brady spiked the ball to stop the clock with seven seconds remaining. New England brought Vinatieri on the field to try a 48-yard kick to win the game.

Vinatieri had been a key part of the Patriots' success with his successful field goals under pressure. Could he come through one more time, with hundreds of millions of people watching around the world? Yes, he could. He

ADAM VINATIERI

Kicker Adam Vinatieri was a big part of the Patriots' success in the 2001 regular season and postseason. He made three game-winning kicks in the regular season, then added two more in the postseason. Vinatieri played college football at South Dakota State. He entered the NFL in 1996, when he signed as an undrafted free agent with the Patriots. Vinatieri would become the only player to ever make field goals in four Super Bowls. He kicked the game-winning field goal in a Super Bowl for New England twice. Vinatieri signed with the Indianapolis Colts before the 2006 season.

drilled the kick as time expired for a 20–17 victory. Patriots players stormed onto the field to celebrate. New England was the Super Bowl champion for the first time in team history.

Super Bowl XXXVI was the first since the September 11, 2001, terrorist attacks on the United States. During the post-game celebration, Patriots owner Robert Kraft shared the victory with the team's fans and

THE PATRIOTS' ADAM VINATIERI STEPS INTO HIS GAME-WINNING 48-YARD KICK AGAINST THE RAMS. NEW ENGLAND'S WIN MARKED THE FIRST TIME A SUPER BOWL HAD ENDED ON THE FINAL PLAY.

the country. "We are the world champions. . . . At this time in our country, we are all Patriots, and tonight the Patriots are champions."

The celebration was especially sweet for the people of New England. They had been waiting for a league title since the team was created more than four decades earlier.

CHAPTER 2

THE BOSTON
PATRIOTS

O

n November 16, 1959, Boston was awarded a professional football team. A group of local businessmen was given the eighth and final team in the new American Football League (AFL). The AFL was a rival league to the more established NFL.

The team was not originally known as the New England Patriots. Instead, they were called the Boston Patriots after locals were allowed to submit ideas for the name. Later, a logo was chosen based on a drawing by an artist from the *Boston Globe* newspaper. The logo was called "Pat Patriot." It showed a minuteman snapping a football. The minutemen were mem-

BILLY SULLIVAN

Massachusetts native Billy Sullivan, an oil executive, was the Patriots' first principal, or main, owner. He initially wanted to purchase the Chicago Cardinals of the NFL. But when the Cardinals moved to St. Louis, Sullivan set his sights on owning the eighth and final AFL team. He was awarded the franchise and put it in Boston. He was inducted into the Patriots Hall of Fame in 2009.

bers of the American colonial militia during the American Revolutionary War (1775–1783)

THE PATRIOTS' GINO CAPPELLETTI POSES IN THE EARLY 1960s. THE WIDE RECEIVER/KICKER LED THE AFL IN SCORING FIVE TIMES.

against Great Britain. The minutemen responded quickly to war threats, thus giving them their name.

With a name and logo chosen, next on the new team's list of needs was a place to play. On April 1, 1960, Boston University's Nickerson Field was selected as the team's first home. It was the former home of the Boston Braves. The Braves NFL team played in Boston from 1932 to 1936. The team moved to Washington DC before the 1937 season and became the Washington Redskins.

In 1960, Boston was excited to have a pro football team again. Lou Saban was chosen to be the Patriots' first coach. He had been a coach at Northwestern and Western Illinois universities.

Former Syracuse University running back Gerhard Schwedes

GINO CAPPELLETTI

One of the most recognizable figures in Patriots history, Gino Cappelletti was a wide receiver and kicker for the team from 1960 to 1970. He was known as "The Duke." Cappelletti was the Patriots' all-time leading scorer until 2005. He was named the AFL's Most Valuable Player (MVP) in 1964 and was voted an AFL all-star five times. Cappelletti was inducted into the Patriots Hall of Fame in 1992. After his playing career was over, Cappelletti became a commentator on the Patriots' radio broadcasts.

was chosen as the squad's first territorial draft choice. Each AFL team had "territorial rights" to a player from its region of the country for a first draft selection. Ron Burton, a running back from Northwestern, was selected as the team's first choice in the official AFL Draft. Burton and Schwedes had a lot of company at training camp. Saban estimated that 350 players tried out for the team before its first season.

The Patriots were placed in the AFL's Eastern Division,

THE PATRIOTS TRY TO TACKLE THE OILERS' BILLY CANNON IN 1961.
BOSTON PLACED SECOND TO HOUSTON IN THE AFL'S EASTERN DIVISION
THAT SEASON AND THE NEXT.

along with the Buffalo Bills, Houston Oilers, and New York Titans. The Titans would eventually change their nickname to Jets. The four teams in the AFL's Western Division were the Dallas Texans, Denver Broncos, Oakland Raiders, and Los Angeles Chargers. The Texans would later move to Kansas City and become the Chiefs. The Chargers would move from Los Angeles to San Diego.

In their first season, the Patriots finished 5–9 and in fourth place in the AFL Eastern Division. They found more success in their second season. They went 9–4–1 and placed second in their division. Boston also finished second, again with a record of 9–4–1, in 1962. The squad would get its first taste of bigger success in 1963.

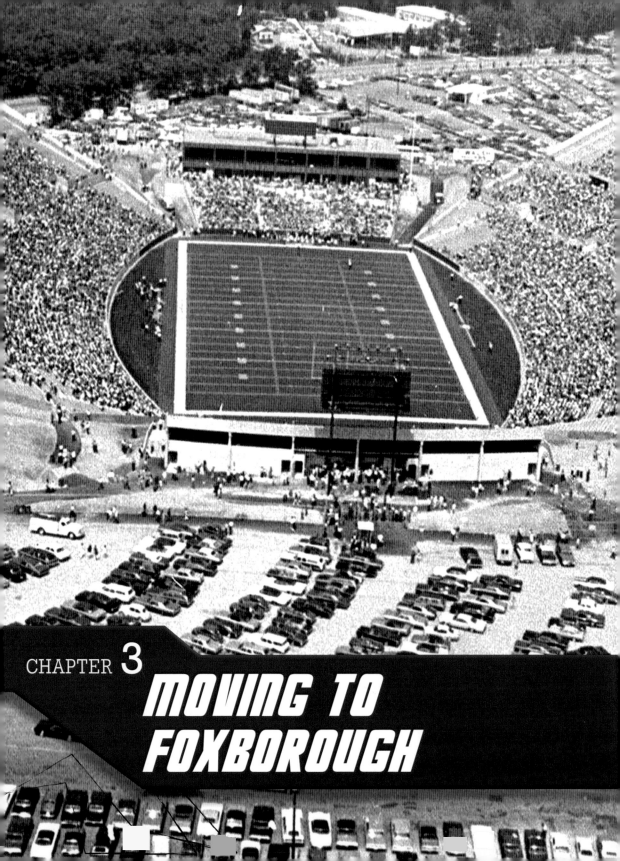

CHAPTER 3

MOVING TO FOXBOROUGH

In 1963, the Patriots moved to Fenway Park, where the Boston Red Sox baseball team played. That year, the Patriots finished just above .500 at 7–6–1. But that record was good enough for them to tie for the AFL's Eastern Division title with the Buffalo Bills.

The Patriots and Bills faced off in a playoff game to decide which team would meet the San Diego Chargers in the AFL Championship Game. Babe Parilli connected with Larry Garron for two touchdowns as visiting Boston beat Buffalo 26–8.

Unfortunately for Boston, the AFL title game would not go nearly as well. The host Chargers crushed the Patriots 51–10 on January 5, 1964. San Diego's Keith Lincoln rushed for 206 yards and a touchdown and added seven catches for 123 yards and a score.

The rest of the 1960s brought mixed results for the Patriots. Some of the team's standouts included wide receiver and kicker Gino Cappelletti,

SCHAEFER STADIUM IS SHOWN IN 1971. IT OPENED THAT YEAR IN FOXBOROUGH, MASSACHUSETTS, AND BECAME THE PATRIOTS' HOME.

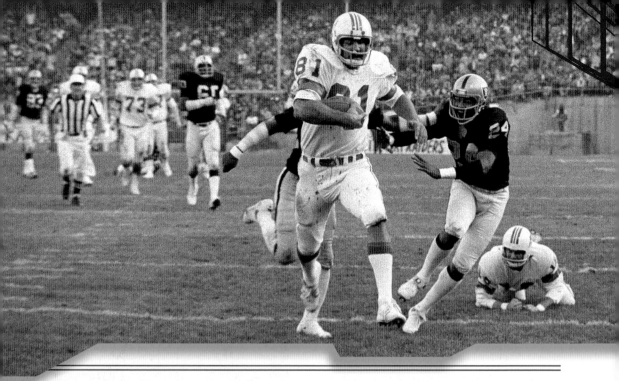

TIGHT END RUSS FRANCIS SCORES ON A 26-YARD TOUCHDOWN RECEPTION IN THE PATRIOTS' 24–21 PLAYOFF LOSS TO THE RAIDERS IN DECEMBER 1976.

through the draft. Among them were guard John Hannah, tight end Russ Francis, quarterback Steve Grogan, and cornerback Mike Haynes. Grogan became the starting quarterback partway through his rookie season in 1975. He replaced Jim Plunkett.

JOHN HANNAH

Called "The Greatest Offensive Lineman of All Time" by Sports Illustrated on the cover of an issue in August 1981, guard John Hannah was a nine-time Pro Bowl selection. He played his entire career with the Patriots, from 1973 to 1985. New England selected him in the first round, fourth overall, in the 1973 NFL Draft. Hannah had been a star at the University of Alabama. He was inducted into the Pro Football Hall of Fame in 1991.

By 1976, enough pieces were in place for New England to go 11–3 and qualify for its first NFL playoff appearance. The Patriots, under coach Chuck Fairbanks, tied the Colts for first place in the division. New England earned a wild-card playoff berth. But the host Oakland Raiders edged the Patriots 24–21 in the first round. Oakland would win the Super Bowl.

The Patriots returned to the playoffs in 1978. That season, the team went 11–5 and captured the first outright division title in team history. The Patriots hosted their first playoff game ever. But they lost 31–14 to the Houston Oilers. After the 1978 season, Fairbanks left to become coach at the University of Colorado. He was replaced by Patriots offensive coordinator Ron Erhardt.

The Patriots were starting to shows signs of progress. The team would knock on the door of big-time success in the 1980s.

STINGLEY'S INJURY

On August 12, 1978, during an exhibition game against the host Oakland Raiders, Patriots wide receiver Darryl Stingley suffered an on-the-field injury that left him paralyzed below his neck.

On the play in which he was injured, Stingley jumped to catch a pass from quarterback Steve Grogan. Stingley and Raiders defensive back Jack Tatum, who also was leaping, collided. No penalty flag was thrown, and even New England's coach at the time, Chuck Fairbanks, said the play was legal.

Tragically, though, the impact of the hit drove several of Stingley's vertebrae together. In time, Stingley regained limited movement in his right arm. He recovered well enough to serve as the Patriots' executive director of player personnel.

In 1983, he published his memoir *Happy to Be Alive*. He died in 2007. His paralysis was a contributing factor, as was bronchial pneumonia.

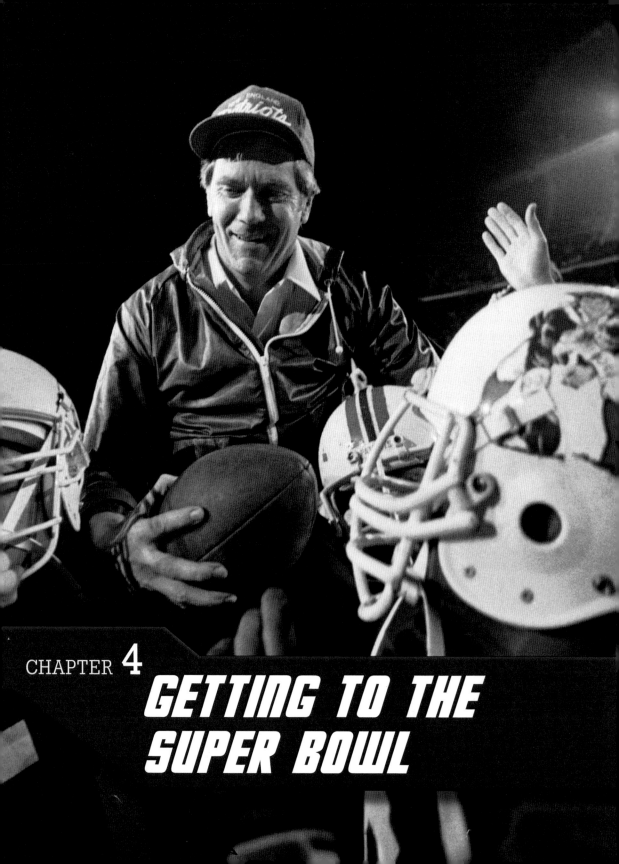

CHAPTER 4

GETTING TO THE SUPER BOWL

The Patriots had their first taste of the NFL playoffs after the 1976 and 1978 seasons. New England also put together solid seasons in 1979 and 1980. The Patriots finished 9–7 and 10–6, respectively. However, each of those two years they just missed going to the playoffs.

New England slumped to 2–14 in 1981 but rebounded in 1982. The season was cut short because of a players' strike. The Patriots finished 5–4 and qualified for a postseason berth. However, they lost 28–13 to the host Miami Dolphins in the first round. New England was still winless in the playoffs in the NFL.

The Patriots finished 8–8 in 1983 and 9–7 in 1984. They fell short of qualifying for the postseason both years. In 1984, New England decided to go with second-year player Tony Eason as its starting quarterback over the aging Steve Grogan.

Eason played well in his first season as the starter. He threw

COACH RAYMOND BERRY IS CARRIED OFF THE FIELD AFTER THE PATRIOTS BEAT THE DOLPHINS 31–14 IN THE AFC TITLE GAME IN JANUARY 1986.

23 touchdown passes with just eight interceptions. New England fired coach Ron Meyer halfway through the season and hired Raymond Berry to replace him. Berry was a Patriots assistant coach from 1978 to 1981. He had enjoyed a Hall of Fame playing career with the Baltimore Colts as a wide receiver from 1955 to 1967.

The 1985 season would be one of the most memorable in Patriots history. Grogan filled in for an ineffective Eason and led New England to six wins in a row before he suffered a broken leg in the eleventh game of the season. Eason became the starter again. The Patriots finished 11–5 and earned a wild-card playoff berth.

QUARTERBACK TONY EASON TAKES A SNAP FROM CENTER RON WOOTEN IN THE PATRIOTS' 27–20 PLAYOFF WIN OVER THE RAIDERS IN JANUARY 1986.

STEVE GROGAN

Patriots quarterback Steve Grogan was known for taking tough hits and enduring numerous injuries. "I tried to play like I was a football player and not just a quarterback," Grogan said.

During his 16-year career, Grogan had five knee operations, three concussions, and several cracked ribs. "He was the kind of guy you wanted to protect, the kind of guy you wanted to play for," Patriots star guard John Hannah said.

Grogan was a former stand-out at Kansas State University. He played for the Patriots his entire NFL career, from 1975 to 1990. Grogan set an NFL record for a quarterback in 1976 with 12 rushing touchdowns. In 1978, the Patriots rushed for an NFL-record 3,165 yards. Grogan ran for 539 of those yards.

Grogan's 16 seasons with New England are a team record.

The Patriots traveled to New York to face the Jets in the first round. Tony Franklin made four field goals to help New England prevail 26–14. The Patriots finally had an NFL playoff win to their credit. Next up was a trip to Los Angeles to face the Raiders. The Raiders had moved from Oakland before the 1982 season. New England won 27–20.

The Patriots then faced their toughest challenge yet. In the AFC Championship Game, New England played the Dolphins at the Orange Bowl in Miami. The Patriots had not won at the Orange Bowl since 1966—in Miami's first season in the AFL.

New England, though, rushed for 255 yards. Craig James led the way with 105. Eason threw for three touchdowns. New England forced Miami star quarterback Dan Marino into a mediocre perfor-mance. The Patriots cruised to a 31–14 victory and a spot in Super Bowl XX.

Awaiting the Patriots on January 26, 1986, at the Superdome in New Orleans, Louisiana, were the mighty Chicago Bears. The Bears went 15–1 in the regular season.

New England proved to be no match for Chicago. The day before the game, Grogan was medically cleared to play. Berry put Grogan in during the second quarter after Eason started 0–for–6. But it did not matter. The Bears were simply too good.

Chicago held New England to 7 rushing yards and inter-cepted two passes by Grogan. The Bears also recorded seven sacks, including a safety, and recovered four fumbles. Chicago rolled to a 46–10 win.

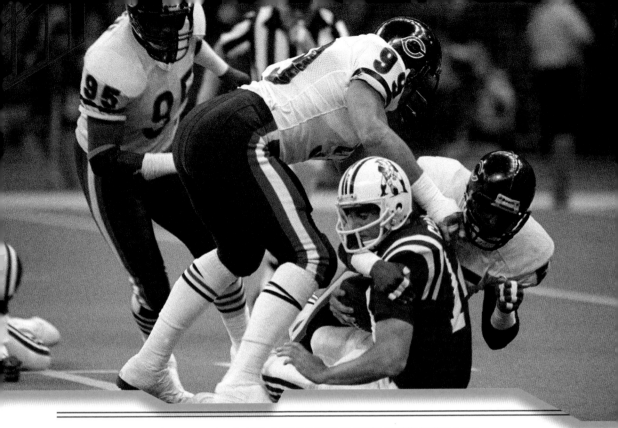

DAN HAMPTON (99) AND OTIS WILSON BRING DOWN NEW ENGLAND QUARTERBACK STEVE GROGAN IN CHICAGO'S 46–10 SUPER BOWL XX WIN.

The next season, New England again finished 11–5 and made the playoffs. This time, the Patriots won the AFC East Division. Eason returned as the starting quarterback. New England traveled to Denver to face the Broncos in the postseason's divisional round. Despite two touchdown tosses from Eason to Stanley Morgan, the Broncos won 22–17. It marked the last time that New England would make the playoffs under Berry. He was fired after the 1989 season.

The 1990s were around the corner. New England had made progress in the 1980s and would make some more in the next decade, though it would not start out well at all.

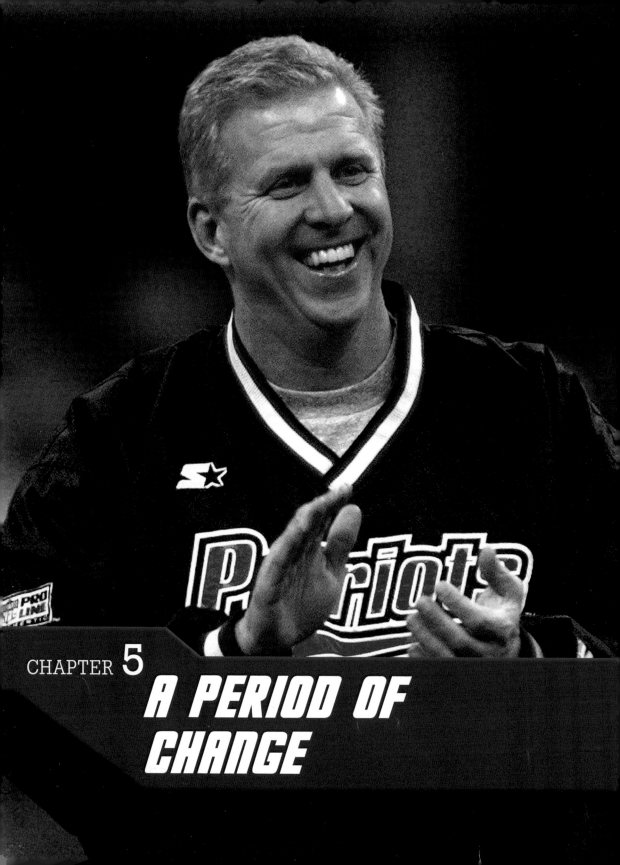

CHAPTER 5

A PERIOD OF CHANGE

The Patriots underwent a lot of changes in the years after their Super Bowl debut in January 1986. The changes left the team with new owners, a new coach, and a new look.

Businessman Billy Sullivan originally brought the Patriots to Massachusetts in 1959. He sold the team for $83 million to businessman Victor Kiam in July 1988. The Patriots suffered through a team-worst 1–15 season in 1990. Kiam sold the team before the 1992 campaign to St. Louis, Missouri, businessman James B. Orthwein.

New England continued to struggle. The team finished 2–14 in 1992. Orthwein then hired Bill Parcells as coach in 1993. Parcells had coached the

ANDRE TIPPETT

Andre Tippett played all 12 of his NFL seasons with the Patriots, from 1982 to 1993. A linebacker who excelled at the pass rush, Tippett set a Patriots record for most sacks over a two-year period with 35 in 1984 and 1985. He entered the Pro Football Hall of Fame in 2008.

BILL PARCELLS COACHED THE PATRIOTS TO SOME SUCCESSFUL SEASONS IN THE 1990s. IN JANUARY 1997, HE LED THE TEAM TO ITS SECOND SUPER BOWL.

New York Giants to two Super Bowl wins. The Patriots also announced that instead of red being the primary color of their uniforms, blue and silver would be featured. The uniforms would also have a new team logo. The makeover was completed when the team selected quarterback Drew Bledsoe with the No. 1 pick in the 1993 NFL Draft. Bledsoe had been a star at Washington State University.

In 1994, Orthwein threatened to sell the team and move it out of New England. Eventually, he sold the Patriots to Boston businessman Robert Kraft for $172 million. Kraft kept the team in New England.

Meanwhile, the Patriots showed improvement under Parcells. They went 5–11 in 1993 before going 10–6 in 1994. They made the playoffs for the first time since 1986. However, New England lost 20–13 to the host Cleveland Browns in the wild-card round.

The Patriots fell back to 6–10 in 1995 but finished 11–5 in 1996 and won the AFC East. Bledsoe threw for 27 touchdowns. Second-year running back Curtis Martin rushed for 1,152 yards and had 17 total touchdowns.

The host Patriots defeated the Pittsburgh Steelers 28–3 in the divisional round and the Jacksonville Jaguars 20–6 in the AFC Championship Game. The Patriots clinched a spot in Super Bowl XXXI at the Superdome in New Orleans. They would face the Green Bay Packers.

Green Bay had big stars in quarterback Brett Favre and defensive end Reggie White. New England battled, though. The Packers led 27–14 at halftime.

NEW ENGLAND'S CURTIS MARTIN RUNS FOR AN 18-YARD TOUCHDOWN IN
SUPER BOWL XXXI. THE PATRIOTS LOST 35–21 TO THE PACKERS.

Martin's 18-yard touchdown run in the third quarter made the score 27–21. But Green Bay's Desmond Howard returned the following kickoff 99 yards for a score. The Packers won 35–21.

Parcells had fought with Kraft over Parcells's desire to have control over team roster decisions. He would end up leaving to become the New York Jets' coach and general manager.

PATS-JETS SAGA

The New York Jets had struggled to a combined 4–28 record in 1995 and 1996. The Jets wanted Patriots coach Bill Parcells to become their coach and general manager.

However, Parcells's contract with New England did not allow him to coach another team. The Jets tried to get around this by making Parcells's top Patriots assistant, secondary coach Bill Belichick, the head coach and saying Parcells was an "adviser."

The Patriots threatened to take legal action against Parcells and the Jets. The NFL stepped in and arranged a deal. New England would release Parcells from his contract so he could become New York's coach and general manager. But the Jets had to give the Patriots four draft picks, including a first-rounder.

Belichick went with Parcells to become the Jets' assistant head coach/secondary coach. He returned to New England as head coach in 2000 and enjoyed a lot of success.

The Patriots hired Pete Carroll as their next coach. He had been the Jets' coach in 1994. New England went 10–6 in 1997 and won the AFC East again. The Patriots lost 7–6 to host Pittsburgh in the playoffs. In 1998, the Patriots finished 9–7 and fell to host Jacksonville 25–10 in the wild-card round. New England went 8–8 in 1999. Kraft fired Carroll.

In January 2000, the Patriots named Jets assistant head coach Bill Belichick, a former defensive assistant of New England's, as head coach. New England was about to begin its most successful period in team history. Belichick would be a big reason why.

BILL BELICHICK SPEAKS ON JANUARY 27, 2000, AT A NEWS CONFERENCE IN WHICH THE PATRIOTS ANNOUNCED THAT THEY HAD HIRED HIM AS THEIR COACH.

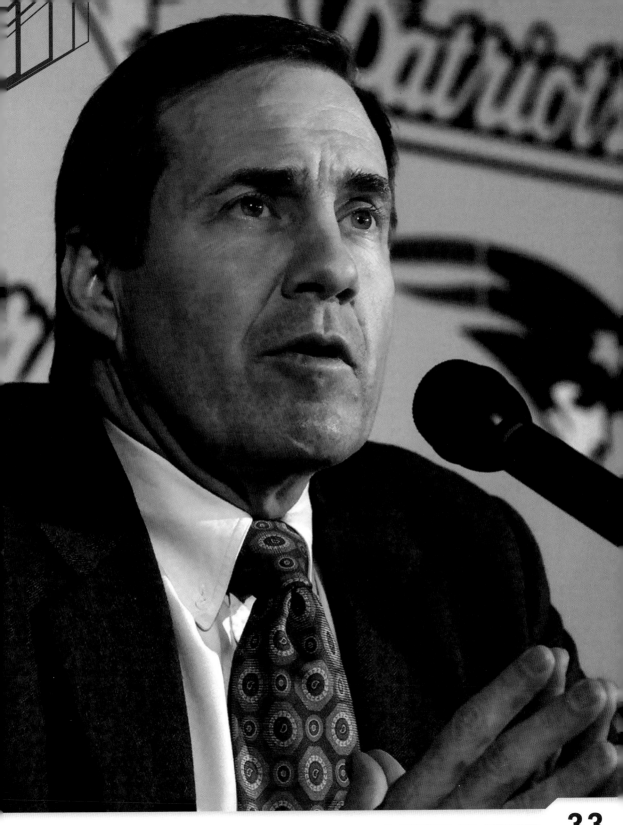

CHAPTER 6

TEAM OF THE DECADE

As the twenty-first century began, the NFL's ultimate prize—a league title—had remained out of the Patriots' reach. That all changed in the new decade. This was in large part because of two men: Bill Belichick and Tom Brady.

New England hired Belichick as coach on January 27, 2000. He had served once before as an NFL head coach—with the Cleveland Browns from 1991 to 1995. The Browns had just one playoff victory during that time. Belichick fared better as a defensive assistant. This included stints with the New York Giants and the Patriots. He served a one-year stint as assistant head coach/secondary coach with New England in 1996. He was the New York Jets' assistant head coach/secondary coach when the Patriots hired him in 2000.

New England went 5–11 in 2000. But the 2001 season was a surprise success. Brady stepped in at quarterback and led New England to its first Super Bowl win—a 20–17 victory over the

WIDE RECEIVER DAVID GIVENS CELEBRATES DURING A 24–21 WIN OVER PHILADELPHIA IN FEBRUARY 2005 THAT GAVE NEW ENGLAND ITS THIRD SUPER BOWL TITLE IN FOUR YEARS.

St. Louis Rams. Brady was chosen as the game's MVP.

The Patriots continued to accomplish incredible things for the rest of the decade.

New England went 9–7 in 2002 and just missed making the postseason. The Patriots really hit their stride in 2003, going 14–2. In the playoffs, host New England beat the Tennessee Titans 17–14 and the Indianapolis Colts 24–14. This put the Patriots in the Super Bowl against the Carolina Panthers.

New England had a fight on its hands in Super Bowl XXXVIII

GILLETTE STADIUM

The Patriots' sparkling new home, Gillette Stadium, opened in 2002 in Foxborough, Massachusetts. It replaced Foxboro Stadium, which had been the team's home since 1971. Foxboro Stadium was demolished in early 2002. Gillette Stadium was built right next to where Foxboro Stadium had stood.

on February 1, 2004, at Reliant Stadium in Houston, Texas. Carolina quarterback Jake Delhomme's 12-yard touchdown pass to Ricky Proehl with 1:08 left tied the score at 29–29.

Brady coolly led the Patriots into field-goal range. Adam Vinatieri drilled a 41-yard kick with four seconds left to put New England ahead 32–29. That would be the final score. Brady passed for 354 yards and three touchdowns. He was named Super Bowl MVP a second time.

The word *dynasty* was being used to describe the Patriots. A talented, smart group of players surrounded Brady. Among them were running back Kevin Faulk, wide receiver Troy Brown, defensive end Richard Seymour, linebackers Tedy Bruschi, Willie McGinest, and Mike Vrabel, and safety Rodney Harrison.

ADAM VINATIERI REACTS AFTER MAKING A LAST-SECOND FIELD GOAL IN
NEW ENGLAND'S 32–29 VICTORY OVER CAROLINA IN SUPER BOWL XXXVIII.

In 2004, the Patriots again went 14–2. New England had acquired running back Corey Dillon from the Cincinnati Bengals before the season. He ran for 1,635 yards. In the playoffs, New England beat visiting Indianapolis 20–3 to set up a showdown with Pittsburgh. The visiting Patriots intercepted rookie

LINEBACKER MIKE VRABEL, WHO SOMETIMES PLAYED ON OFFENSE FOR THE PATRIOTS, MAKES A 2-YARD TOUCHDOWN CATCH AGAINST THE EAGLES IN SUPER BOWL XXXIX.

quarterback Ben Roethlisberger three times and won 41–27.

New England was back in the Super Bowl, this time against the Philadelphia Eagles. Super Bowl XXXIX was held on February 6, 2005, at Alltel Stadium in Jacksonville, Florida. New England took a 10-point lead in the fourth quarter with the help of a 2-yard touchdown run by Dillon. The Patriots held on and won 24–21. New England wide receiver Deion Branch was the game's MVP. He had 11 catches for 133 yards.

The Patriots had won three Super Bowls in four seasons. They became just the second team to do that, joining the Dallas Cowboys of the 1990s.

New England made winning Super Bowls look easier than it actually was.

In 2005, the Patriots finished 10–6 but were knocked out by the host Denver Broncos 27–13 in the playoffs' divisional round. In 2006, New England went 12–4 but lost 38–34 as host Indianapolis and star quarterback Peyton Manning rallied in the AFC title game.

Before the 2007 season, the Patriots traded a fourth-round draft pick to the Oakland Raiders for wide receiver Randy Moss. Moss was talented but had gotten into some trouble off the field.

However, the deal paid off when Moss displayed a more mature attitude. New England became the first NFL team to finish a regular season 16–0. The Miami Dolphins went 14–0 in 1972, before the NFL went to a 16-game schedule in 1978.

New England scored an NFL-record 589 points. Brady established a league mark with 50 touchdown throws. Moss made an NFL-record 23 touchdown receptions.

The Patriots would try to join the 1972 Dolphins as the only NFL teams to finish an entire season—regular season and postseason—undefeated. Host New England beat the Jacksonville Jaguars 31–20 and the San Diego Chargers 21–12 in the playoffs. The Patriots would play in a fourth Super Bowl in seven seasons.

Squaring off against the Patriots were the New York Giants, a wild-card team. New England was a big favorite going into Super Bowl XLII on February 3, 2008, at University of Phoenix Stadium in Glendale, Arizona.

The game was close throughout, though. Brady's 6-yard scoring pass to Moss gave the Patriots a 14–10 advantage with 2:42 remaining. Quarterback Eli Manning then guided the Giants on an 83-yard drive. It was capped with Manning's 13-yard touchdown pass to wide receiver Plaxico Burress with 35 seconds left. New York took a 17–14 lead.

"SPYGATE"

The Patriots' remarkable 2007 season was not without controversy. The NFL disciplined New England after it was revealed that the team, from its sideline, had videotaped the New York Jets defensive coaches' signals during a game on September 9. The NFL fined coach Bill Belichick $500,000 and the team $250,000 and took away a first-round draft pick in 2008.

The Patriots got the ball back but could not move it. The Giants won 17–14. "We shocked the world but not ourselves," New York linebacker Antonio Pierce said.

In 2008, Brady suffered a knee injury in the opening game. He would miss the rest of the season. Behind backup quarterback Matt Cassel, New England finished 11–5 and tied Miami atop the AFC East standings. However, the Dolphins made the playoffs and the Patriots did not because of a tiebreaker.

GIANTS DEFENSIVE END MICHAEL STRAHAN PRESSURES PATRIOTS
QUARTERBACK TOM BRADY IN SUPER BOWL XLII. NEW YORK WON 17–14
TO PREVENT NEW ENGLAND FROM COMPLETING A PERFECT SEASON.

Brady was back in 2009. The 10–6 Patriots won the AFC East. Brady, though, was intercepted three times as the visiting Baltimore Ravens surprisingly dominated New England in a 33–14 wild-card win.

The decade was over. The Patriots had won three Super Bowls and came close to winning another. The team had not captured a league title before that decade. But the Patriots were big-time winners when it ended. That span alone produced many memories for the team's fans to cherish for a lifetime.

TIMELINE

1959	Boston is awarded the eighth and final team in the new AFL on November 16.
1960	After a public contest, the team is officially named the Patriots and the team colors of red, white, and blue are chosen on February 20.
1960	The Patriots lose 13–10 to the visiting Denver Broncos in their first regular-season game on September 9.
1964	The Patriots lose to the San Diego Chargers 51–10 in the AFL Championship Game on January 5.
1970	The AFL and the NFL officially merge to form a larger NFL.
1970	It is announced on April 4 that the Patriots will move to Schaefer Stadium (later known as Sullivan Stadium and Foxboro Stadium) in Foxborough, Massachusetts—outside Boston—for the 1971 season.
1971	The Boston Patriots are renamed the New England Patriots on March 22.
1976	On December 18, the Patriots lose in their first playoff game, 24–21 at Oakland.
1986	After earning their first NFL playoff victories with three road wins, the Patriots play in their first Super Bowl on January 26. New England loses 46–10 to the Chicago Bears at the Superdome in New Orleans, Louisiana.
1993	Former New York Giants coach Bill Parcells is named the coach of the Patriots on January 21.

1997	New England loses 35–21 to the Green Bay Packers in Super Bowl XXXI on January 26 in the Superdome.
2000	Former New England assistant coach Bill Belichick is named the Patriots' coach on January 27.
2002	The Patriots, with second-year quarterback Tom Brady leading the way, win their first NFL title with a 20–17 victory over the St. Louis Rams in Super Bowl XXXVI on February 3 at the Superdome.
2002	The Gillette Company receives the naming rights to the Patriots' new stadium, resulting in it being named Gillette Stadium on August 5.
2004	New England defeats the Carolina Panthers 32–29 on February 1 in Super Bowl XXXVIII at Reliant Stadium in Houston, Texas.
2005	The Patriots beat the Philadelphia Eagles 24–21 in Super Bowl XXXIX on February 6 at Alltel Stadium in Jacksonville, Florida. It is New England's third Super Bowl win in four seasons.
2007	On December 29, New England becomes the first team in NFL history to finish a regular season 16–0 with a 38–35 win over the host New York Giants.
2008	The Giants upset the Patriots 17–14 in Super Bowl XLII on February 3 at University of Phoenix Stadium in Glendale, Arizona.
2010	Brady is intercepted three times as the Patriots are surprisingly routed 33–14 by the visiting Baltimore Ravens in a wild-card playoff game on January 10.

FRANCHISE HISTORY
Boston Patriots (1960–70)
New England Patriots (1971–)

SUPER BOWLS
(wins in bold)
1985 (XX), 1996 (XXXI), **2001 (XXXVI)**, **2003 (XXXVIII)**, **2004 (XXXIX)**, 2007 (XLII)

AFL CHAMPIONSHIP GAMES
(1960–69)
1963

AFC CHAMPIONSHIP GAMES
(since 1970 AFL-NFL merger)
1985, 1996, 2001, 2003, 2004, 2006, 2007

DIVISION CHAMPIONSHIPS
(since 1970 AFL-NFL merger)
1978, 1986, 1996, 1997, 2001, 2003, 2004, 2005, 2006, 2007, 2009

KEY PLAYERS
(position, seasons with team)
Drew Bledsoe (QB, 1993–2001)
Tom Brady (QB, 2000–)
Tedy Bruschi (LB, 1996–2008)
Nick Buoniconti (LB, 1962–1968)
Gino Cappelletti (K/WR, 1960–70)
Steve Grogan (QB, 1975–90)
John Hannah (G, 1973–85)
Mike Haynes (CB, 1976–82)
Ty Law (CB, 1995–2004)
Stanley Morgan (WR, 1977–89)
Andre Tippett (LB, 1982–93)
Adam Vinatieri (K, 1996–2005)

KEY COACHES
Bill Belichick (2000–):
    112–48–0; 14–4 (playoffs)
Raymond Berry (1984–89):
    48–39–0; 3–2 (playoffs)
Bill Parcells (1993–96):
    32–32–0; 2–2 (playoffs)

HOME FIELDS
Gillette Stadium (2002–)
Foxboro Stadium (1971–2001)
    Known as Sullivan Stadium
    (1983–89) and Schaefer Stadium
    (1971–82)
Harvard Stadium (1970)
Alumni Stadium (1969)
Fenway Park (1963–68)
Nickerson Field (1960–62)

* All statistics through 2009 season

New England coach Bill Belichick was not the first coach in his family. His father, Steve, played fullback for the Detroit Lions in 1941 and scouted and served as an assistant coach for the U.S. Naval Academy team for 33 years. He also wrote a book in 1962 called *Football Scouting Mechanics* that became essential reading for other scouts.

"If they want you to cook the dinner, at least they ought to let you shop for some of the groceries."
—Former New England coach Bill Parcells, on his desire to have control over deciding which players were on the team. When he could not gain such power with the Patriots, he left to become the New York Jets' coach and general manager in 1997.

"At the risk of sounding immodest, I believe we are the team of the decade."
—Patriots owner Robert Kraft, on his team's success in the 2000s

On December 12, 1982, a snowstorm hit New England during the Patriots' game against the Miami Dolphins at Schaefer Stadium. The playing conditions were terrible. The score was still tied at 0–0 with 4:45 left when Patriots kicker John Smith prepared to attempt a 33-yard field goal. During a break in the action, New England coach Ron Meyer ordered snowplow operator Mark Henderson to clear a spot on the field. He did, and Smith converted the kick. Matt Cavanaugh was the holder. Dolphins coach Don Shula protested furiously. But the kick stood. New England would go on to win 3–0. The contest is now referred to as the "snowplow game." In 1983, the NFL banned the use of snowplows on the field.

GLOSSARY

American Football Conference

One of two conferences that make up the NFL. As of 2010, there were 16 teams in the AFC, as it is commonly referred to.

American Football League

A professional football league that operated from 1960 to 1969 before merging with the National Football League.

berth

A place, spot, or position, such as in the NFL playoffs.

draft

A system used by professional sports leagues to select new players in order to spread incoming talent among all teams.

dynasty

A team that wins a lot of games, usually including more than one league championship, over a time spanning multiple seasons.

franchise

An entire sports organization, including the players, coaches, and staff.

general manager

The executive who is in charge of the team's overall operation. He or she hires and fires coaches, drafts college players, and signs free agents.

postseason

Games played in the playoffs by the top teams after the regular-season schedule has been completed.

Pro Bowl

A game after the regular season in which the top players from the AFC play against the top players from the NFC.

rookie

A first-year professional athlete.

sack

Term used when a defensive player tackles the quarterback behind the line of scrimmage.